Dream Out Loud

Dream Out Loud

21 Day Path to Your Heart's Desires

Tara Dale

ISBN: 0692596526
ISBN 13: 9780692596524
Library of Congress Control Number: 2015920601
Dream Out Loud, Kentfield, CA

Contents

DREAM OUT LOUD: A Twenty-One-Day Path to Your Heart's Desires, is an activity based workbook designed to give you twenty-one basic principles to use as you manifest your heart's desires.

The reason I say "heart's desires" is because I believe our hearts are much more powerful than our brains. If you want something from your heart, you are coming from a very pure and powerful place, whereas, if you want something from your brain you are coming from a place that is filled with preconceived judgments.

The heart is the master organ in the human body. It is the first organ to develop in a fetus. The Heart Math Institute has created a machine that can measure the electromagnetic energy of the heart. They have concluded that the heart's electromagnetic energy is approximately five thousand times greater than that of the brain. This magnetic field can be measured up to several feet from the body. The brain is an easy target for ego-based desires, as well as programming that you have taken on from the outside world.

Step into your heart and ask it, "What do I want?" Sit back and listen. An answer will come to you immediately. Be patient with yourself, as this skill may take time and repetition, but it will come. These exercises will help you master this innate skill.

If you are brave enough to quiet your mind and listen to your heart, you will be able to follow your heart's desire and create the life you want.

My First Manifestation

I started manifesting when I was in kindergarten. My first big manifestation happened on my way home from school one day. My neighbor drove me home from school. We pulled into the driveway and noticed fifteen horses grazing in my front lawn.

I jumped out of the station wagon, ran into the middle of the horses, and shouted, "You're here!" It was a brief moment, but it was the happiest day of my life at that point. Then my mom ran outside, grabbed my arm, and pulled me into the house, as any protective mother would. She had no idea that I had been wishing for this for over a year. She was afraid that all the horses would trample me.

I sat in the living room and watched the horses through the window. I desperately wanted to go outside, jump on one of the horse's backs, and ride fearlessly down the street with no saddle or bridle.

What had happened the previous year? I was infatuated with horses. My mom had covered my bedroom floor with green burlap to look like a pasture. Every day, I played with toy horses in my room. My mom would take me across the street and down a hill to the stable to feed carrots to the horses. The year kindergarten began, I became more independent and played in the yard. Naturally I would sneak across the street and down the grassy knoll to the stable. I would bring carrots and apples to feed the horses regularly. I would talk to them as I fed them and say, "When you get out, please come get me at 15107 Woodsbluff St." Every time I could sneak away, I'd go to the stable and talk to the horses. I believed wholeheartedly that one day the horses would come and get me. Was what happened on the day of their arrival just a fluke?

On the day the horses came to me, the barn was being repainted. The horses were put in a big corral, and they broke through and escaped.

Was it my desire that made this happen, or was it just a random act? It doesn't matter. The power of wishing and wanting something so deeply that you can feel it in every cell of your body is powerful.

My Experience

For as long as I can remember, I have loved horses. My father supported my dreams by learning to ride with me. I will always cherish the memories of riding with my father.

In my teenage years, I enjoyed riding through the countryside with him. We would gallop through fields and fly over fences.

On Sundays we would ride cross country with a riding club. One day it was particularly cold and icy and a horse slipped over a fence, severely injuring the rider. Our group stopped for a while to help the fallen rider. As I waited, my fingers and feet became numb from the cold. Instead, I felt dread descend over my heart. I did not feel as footloose and fancy free, as I did the previous summer when I had jumped over the same fence. I felt fearful. My father tried to reassure me by saying, "You can do this. Look where you want to go. Focus all of your attention onto the other side of the fence and fly over like you usually do." At that point, I was freezing from the cold and shaking with fear. My father became stern and loud. He looked me in the eyes and said, "Over, under or through Tara. Follow me." He jumped over the fence. I stayed on the other side crying. I told him I could not do it. This time in a louder, more serious voice he repeated, "Focus on where you want to go and get over, under, or through this fence NOW!"

I took a few deep breaths to compose myself, and a moment to connect with my horse. I focused on the easy feeling I felt the previous summer as I flew over the fence. I kept my full attention on where I wanted to land on the other side. I made it over safely and we galloped away to catch up with the group.

It felt so good to face my fear. I was grateful I made it over safely.

The quote, "Over, under or through" holds special meaning between my father and I. Every time I accomplish something momentous, my father sends me flowers with a note, "Over, under or through."

Life as an Adult

After college, when it was time to get a "real job," I followed my brain, which told me to be safe, work in an office like everyone else and make enough money to pay rent.

One day, a man came into our office and did a quick workshop on creating the life of your dreams. It was a teaser for signing up for a Tony Robbins event. I really enjoyed the exercises. It was the first time in a long while that I felt as if I had tapped into my creativity and heart. He asked me, "If you could do anything, what would you do?" I decided then that I would start my own business. I called it, Lifestyle Fitness. My intention was to inspire people who did not like fitness to begin enjoying exercise and healthy eating.

A few years later, I bought my first home. It had a studio downstairs off the garden. Here I created my first yoga studio, called the *Inner Garden.*

After a couple of years of enjoying working with my private clients, I was craving more community with my peers. Sitting on the deck with my dog Wilbur, gazing at the sky I wondered, *"what's next?"*

The next day, someone contacted me and said, "There is a man named Tim who wants to open a yoga studio and he's looking to partner with a yoga instructor."

The next day, I met him at a site that he was hoping to make into a yoga studio. I loved the space and thought it would be a fun project. He told me to get back to him with a business plan.

I had never written a business plan before. I went home and wrote all of my visions for my dream yoga studio in a report. My main premise was based upon the following saying, "there are many rivers to the ocean." Two days later, we created a partnership and named the studio Yoga Tree. This studio on Stanyan St. in San Francisco was our first of nine studios in the Bay Area. We became known for having the best teachers in town. We were also one of the first studios to have many different styles of yoga under one roof.

I encouraged our teachers to complete at least sixty hours of continuing education per year to stay strong leaders. Later, with the help of my friend Darren Main, we created two-hundred, five-hundred and one-thousand hour, world-renowned teacher-training programs. This success was beyond my dreams.

Why Write a Workbook?

All my life, I have believed that life is magical. I knew my heart spoke louder than my brain. To me a world that put everyone in the same box didn't make sense.

I became very confused when my brain developed a voice. This happens to all of us around puberty. Do you remember when you were younger and just enjoyed life without thinking about all of the "should' s" and "shouldn't' s"? At what age did you begin to allow your brain to stop you from following your heart?

It took many years to learn that I have two voices, my brain and my heart. While I'm grateful for my brain, I believe that following my heart allowed me to create my amazing life.

I am writing this book in order to help others come out of the small, boxed-up reality they may have bought into and realize that life is much more expansive! You can have all of your heart's desires.

Go for it! Figure out what you want in your heart, believe in your vision, and have faith that it is happening. Have faith that you are supported by an invisible superpower. Take action each day to make your dreams a reality.

Am I special? Yes, and so are you! We all have the power to manifest our heart's desires. Manifesting requires pure heartfelt motivation, vision, belief and, of course, action.

Sometimes action does not immediately create the desired results in the way you are expecting. Be open. Magic will happen.

By taking action toward your desire or vision every day, you are telling the universe that you are serious about your desire.

This workbook is intended to help you clarify your vision, as well as give you tools to manifest purely and rapidly. The time to listen to your powerful heart is now!

YouTube

After I wrote this workbook, I decided to search on YouTube for people who believed in the idea that, like your brain, your heart can communicate with you.

YouTube is an amazing resource for continuing education. I started listening to many of the authors who have inspired me over the past few decades. I have watched hundreds of videos.

I have added an activity each day, titled, "YouTube Video" to accompany the workbook. Go to YouTube.com, find my channel, "Dream Out Loud with Tara", and go to the playlist tab. You can listen to or watch the clip I have chosen. Subscribe and browse my playlists that are full of great videos.

You have options. If you don't have time during the day, it's a great idea to put on headphones at night and listen before bed. If some of the videos I have selected are too long for you to listen to each day, search for another that is applicable and shorter. You can also just listen to ten minutes or so and decide whether you'd like to add it to your watch later list.

Write one sentence or more about what inspired you from each video under the notes section at the end of each chapter.

Color

This workbook is meant to be action oriented and creative. Take time to read the chapters and do the exercises. Get into a space that feels magical to you.

Each chapter has a coloring aspect. Coloring helps you disconnect from your day and access your creative mind. Coloring utilizes both hemispheres of the brain—right and left. Coloring will help enhance your focus, creativity, and concentration. It is also a great way to quiet the chatter of your mind. It can invoke the feeling from childhood when you just did something for the pure joy of it. Color the quote drawings while holding your intention in your heart. Notice how it helps you to relax and get into a creative space. Be a child again and color.

Daily Activities

Create a sacred space for your creativity to flow. Light a candle and then set up your markers, your workbook, a journal or some blank pieces of paper.

Exercise

It is helpful to get your body moving. You can try exercising for at least 5 minutes before you start reading and doing the activities in this workbook. I like to take a brisk walk or practice yoga to get my energy flowing so I can be in a fresh space to create.

Relax and clear your mind-

Sit for a couple of minutes and meditate, lay down, cover your eyes and listen to a guided meditation, or any other practice that helps you clear your mind.

I have created a special guided meditation that takes 15 minutes. The nice thing about guided meditation is, you can lie down on your back and just let go. Please give it a try. If it works for you please use this daily.

Get Started

This is the first video of your journey.

Guided meditation for energy and manifesting your desires. Posted by "Dream out loud with Tara. Published on May 22, 2016.

https://youtu.be/q5hJ0WZLoUs

Supplies (optional)

Here are some examples:

Special pen
Journal or notebook
Colored crayons, markers, or paint
Candles
Sage, incense, or essential oils in a diffuser
Nonflammable pot or bowl for burning negative beliefs written on a piece of paper
Collection of magazines or pictures
Poster or corkboards for a collage

YouTube Video

5 Things Successful People Do—Mindset Monday." by "FitLifeTV." October 20, 2014.
https://youtu.be/Em1uXKaezPI.

Notes

The only thing stronger than fear is Love. Have courage to follow your Heart!

-unknown

Follow Joy

JOY ARISES WHEN you let your heart lead. You're capable of creating anything you desire. What makes you happy? Ask your heart what it desires. As you open your heart, you will find the answer.

There are many techniques that help you connect with and open your heart. Try this one: lie down and cover your eyes or sit up straight with your feet on the floor with your eyes closed. Take your hands and hold them softly on your heart. Take a couple of deep breaths. Now feel your heart and take eight breaths directly into your heart and upper back, as if you're breathing into your heart and creating space for it to open up. How often do you pay attention to the back of your heart? Feel the tender spot in your upper back behind your heart. This sacred area is powerful and receptive. Breathe into it lovingly. Stay with your breath and think of something or someone you're deeply grateful for. Now, think of something that you appreciate about yourself. Smile softly and lovingly as you allow the energy of gratitude and appreciation to fill every cell of your body. This is a powerful activity that works quickly. I recommend doing it for at least three minutes. If three minutes feels too long for you, try one minute. If you'd like to practice longer, go for it. I recommend doing this practice every day before you do the activities in this workbook.

When you are happy, you inspire others to be happy. Find your happiness and joy, and it will radiate. The path of your heart holds magic.

Action

It all starts with a vision. What's yours?

For at least eight minutes, write about everything in your life that makes you happy.

Now, write about your desire. What is it that you want? This will be your focus for many of the activities in this workbook. It can evolve and even change as you progress through this workbook.

Be curious. What makes you feel joyful? Identify what you are truly passionate about and go for it. If you have an idea or desire that inspires you, make it happen.

Daydream throughout the day about what it feels like living in your desired reality.

YouTube video

"The Little Red Book That Makes Your Dreams Come True"! (Unknown Author) - Law of Attraction. Posted by "YouAreCreators2." October 1, 2015. https://youtu.be/Fiv2J1eITdM

Notes

FOLLOW YOUR
BLISS AND THE
UNIVERSE WILL
OPEN DOORS
WHERE THERE
WERE ONLY
WALLS.

- Joseph Campbell

Clarity

CLARITY IS ONE of the most important steps when manifesting your desires. When you have clarity, your desires will flow to you easier. Get clear about what it is that you want to manifest.

Make goals and decisions that are consistent with your vision. Know what or who is important to you in your life now. Knowing your priorities helps you to create your plan. For whatever you decide to create, remember to generate it from your heart. If more money is something you desire, figure out a strategy from your heart. Ask yourself, why or for what purpose do you desire this? As Michael Franti sings in one of his songs, "Do it for the love, not for money." It is perfectly fine to make a lot of money. The trick is to love what you are doing. With love, passion, and action, the money will come.

As you do these exercises, please connect with and follow your heart–it is your magic wand. As I stated earlier, heart waves are thousands of times more powerful than brain waves.

Create your desires from your heart.

Action

Write about what you are creating. It is fine if your desire changes as you become clearer this week.

Close your eyes and feel your heart. Feel your heart open and expand. As you connect with your heart, ask, "What are my true desires?"

Write down everything that comes to you from your heart for at least eight minutes. Do not censor your thoughts.

YouTube Video
"Why Clarity of Vision is Crucial to Achieve Your Goals." Posted by "John Assaraf." April 26, 2013. https://youtu.be/ZAq3SvGoSP8.

Notes

When you have clarity of intention, the universe conspires with you to make it happen.

- Fabianne Fredrickson

DAY 3

Celebrate

CELEBRATE YOUR PAST creations. When you celebrate things you have created in the past, you infuse your body, mind, and spirit with creative energy. What have you created? Send gratitude to yourself and the universe for having manifested these desires. Honor yourself for all you have created so far. This internal gratitude will inspire you to make an even bigger contribution to yourself and to the world. When you focus on what you have achieved, the energy will help you manifest and bless your future accomplishments. You have so much to be grateful for. Soak in the loving feeling of gratitude.

As you attain your new desires, celebrate each step of your process. Get excited about what you are creating. Jump for joy as you create more of your heart's desires. This energy will inspire you!

Action

Make a list of things you have created that make you proud. Honor yourself for creating these things. As you move forward with new desires, celebrate each step.

YouTube Video

Vlog - Power of Play" Posted by "Sonia Choquette"." December 11, 2014.
  https://youtu.be/NOLDMWQA1UQ

Notes

The more you praise and celebrate life, the more there is in life to celebrate.

~Oprah Winfrey

DAY 4

Help Others

YOU CAN CHANGE the world. There is a deep and expansive joy that comes from helping others.

When your desire enhances the lives of others, it flows faster to you. Enjoy how good it feels to get what you want while helping others at the same time.

What do you want to contribute to the world? How will your desire help others? Consider how you can use your unique talents to help others and make the world an even better place. It is not necessary for you to be like Mother Theresa. If your desire is to be successful in real estate, you can help others by finding the right home for them. If you want to make a film, you are in turn providing people with entertainment. Even buying a new car will positively affect your family and additionally will help the sales person make a living. If your desire helps others, it is sure to be a success.

Action

Write a list, story, or paragraph about how your desire will help others.

Extra credit

Help someone every day. You can help elderly person to put their groceries into their car or to cross the street, or to make dinner for a friend who is ill or overly busy. By helping someone you will enhance your energy. Notice how great it feels to help someone.

YouTube Video

"You are amazing - make your dreams come true". Posted by Anthony Beardsell.
Jan 14, 2015.
https://youtu.be/N47vTVbv4ms

Notes

We rise
by
lifting
others.

-Robert Ingersoll

DAY 5

Thoughts

THE LAW OF Attraction states, "Like energy attracts like energy." You create your reality with your thoughts, feelings, beliefs, and actions. Thoughts are energy. Thoughts create your reality. What you think to be true in your subconscious mind becomes your reality. Keep all thoughts positive! Chapter seven will teach you techniques on how to rephrase negative thoughts into positive beliefs.

My father told me a Cherokee Native American Legend about two wolves.

A wise old Native American and his grandson were sitting by the fire. The old man said, "There are two wolves that live inside you, one is good, the other is bad." The grandson asked, "What are they doing there?" The grandfather replied, "They are fighting each other." He continued, "The good one is your love, peace, joy, empathy, compassion, faith, and truth. The bad one is your fear, anger, envy, resentment, and superiority." The grandson asked, "Which one will win?" The grandfather replied, "The one that you feed."

This story signifies the power of the mind. We are all capable of greatness, as well as destruction. Whatever you focus the power of your mind on will create your reality. Your thoughts are alive. Each thought you entertain emits a corresponding energy vibration. Your thoughts, beliefs, and actions create your reality. Control your conscious and subconscious mind to transform your life.

Action

List the positive, life-affirming videos, TV shows or music that you listen to as well as the books and papers you read. How do they make you feel?

Write down all of the positive, supportive interactions you had today. How did they make you feel? Were any interactions today unsupportive? If so, how did they make you feel?

YouTube Video

"The Magic In Your Mind - Learn The Secrets of Success! (Law Of Attraction)"
Posted by "YouAreCreators2." January 11, 2016.
https://youtu.be/DEs6VlbMrQs

Notes

Whether you think you can, or you think you can't, you are right.

- Henry Ford

DAY 6

Release

LOVE AND FEAR are two of the most powerful emotions. Negative beliefs can be programmed into our subconscious by our own thought processes, as well as the beliefs of others.

Surround yourself with positive, optimistic people. Avoid sharing your dreams with those who are negative or fearful. It is important to only share your heart's desires with those who want the best for you. Keep your dreams secret from those who may be jealous or who tell you that you can't succeed. Protect your dream garden. It is fun to share your dreams with people who are one hundred percent supportive and positive. I have found that it is usually best to keep your desires a secret until they have become a reality. This way, you can grow your dreams with confidence, knowing that only your positive energy is feeding and nourishing them.

It is vital that you keep your thoughts and feelings positive. It is natural to have fears. When fears arise, know that they are illusions. Some fears keep you safe from harm.

There are many acronyms for fear:

False experiences appearing real

Forget everything and run

Face everything and rejoice

I prefer the third saying.

Look at each fear and determine if it is real or not. You have the control and ability to release your fears.

As you release thoughts and feelings of fear, replace them with positive statements. (This is covered in the next chapter.)

Action

Release and burn all negative beliefs.

Take a moment to sit in a quiet place and visualize what you want. Ask yourself why you believe you can't have what you want.

For at least eight minutes, write down all of your negative beliefs on paper with a pen or marker. Expel every negative thought onto the paper, even if your brain tries to use reality as an excuse for why your dream is not possible. Example: I'm not rich enough, I'm not pretty enough, or heart magic doesn't work for me.

Get a pot or nonflammable bowl. Tear up the sheet of paper that contains all of your negative beliefs. You may add sage or any other herbs to the burning pot. As you watch the flames engulf and burn your negative thoughts, say a personal mantra, such as, "I now burn and release all negative thoughts and beliefs. I release their power over me. I am now creating my heart's desire."

Repeat the mantra until the paper turns completely to ash.

Repeat this exercise until you truly believe in your heart that all negative beliefs have been released.

YouTube Video

"F.E.A.R." Nelson Rivera Jr, November 4, 2014.
   https://youtu.be/K-09ZN86huI

Notes

DAY 7

Rephrase

IF YOU HEAR yourself saying, "I can never create," or anything else negative, stop now. Rephrase what you do want in the present as the following: "I am now creating…"

It is normal for your mind to have doubts and negative undertones. Our brains only know what they have been programmed to know and often times the world tells us to doubt our power.

Take control of your thoughts. Each time you notice yourself thinking or saying something that does not support your desire, acknowledge it lovingly. Tell the fear that you are safe.

Rephrase negative thoughts into positive thoughts. If you hear yourself say something that does not support your dreams, stop, notice, and rephrase. This will be a lifelong practice.

If your brain is having a temper tantrum and you find it difficult to rephrase a doubt or fear into a positive statement, stop, close your eyes, put your hands on your heart, feel your heart's energy, and ask your heart for the truth.

I appreciate the brain very much. Knowledge is power! Again, I believe that the heart is much wiser and more powerful than the brain. By being brave enough to stop negativity and rephrase it in a positive way, you reprogram your mind.

Be proud of yourself for noticing. Have the courage to rephrase negative thoughts into your true desires. Redirect all negativity. Protect your dream by nourishing it and taking out all of the negative mental weeds. Just as weeds take the life force from plants, negative thoughts suck the life force from your dreams. If you believe in your negative thoughts, you give them power. You will create what you believe.

Continue to weed out your dream garden and nourish it with positive affirmations, thoughts, and actions. Each time fear comes up, which is natural, just send love and tell yourself that you're OK. Tell your fears to go speak to the boss, your heart.

Action
Did you catch yourself saying anything negative today? If so, make a list of what you said and rephrase it in a positive way.

YouTube Video
"Stop saying 'I Want,' and Start saying 'I Have!' (Law of Attraction)." Posted by "YouAreCreators." *May 5, 2015.*
   https://youtu.be/fYKs38Wd3iQ

Notes

-Neil Barringham

DAY 8

Love Yourself

IT IS ESSENTIAL to love yourself. In order to manifest or experience loving people and circumstances you need to love yourself first. Loving yourself improves everything in your life, your health, relationships, and your ability to manifest your desires.

You are valuable to yourself and others. The most important relationship you will ever have is with yourself. It is not selfish to love yourself; loving yourself is a healing practice. It allows you to give love to and receive love from other people. The relationships you have with others mirrors aspects of the relationship you have with yourself.

You are enough! Embrace all parts of yourself, even the things you need to work on. You are an important part of this world. Each moment that you are in the place of knowing that you matter, your power ignites.

You are a miracle. You have unique gifts and talents. There is something magical in you that no other person possesses. You are valuable. You are talented. You are amazing. You can make a difference in the world! Feel gratitude for all that you are. Know you are a significant piece of the whole of the universe.

Here is a quote from Nelson Mandela's 1994 inaugural speech:

"Our deepest fear is not that we are inadequate. Our deepest fear is that we are powerful beyond measure. It is our light, not our darkness, that most frightens us. We ask ourselves, who am I to be brilliant, gorgeous, talented, fabulous? But really, who are you not to be? Playing small does not serve the world. There is nothing enlightened about shrinking so that other people won't feel insecure around you. We are born to make manifest the glory that is within us. It is not just in some of us, it is in everyone. As we let our light shine, we unconsciously give other people permission to do the same. As we are liberated from our own fear, our presence automatically liberates others."

Action

Look into the mirror at least three times. Look deeply into your eyes and tell yourself, "I am enough" or say, "I love you". Repeat this process daily until you believe it. This simple exercise is magical and powerful.

Connect with your heart to see if you believe this. If you do, then you had easy homework today. If you don't, take a moment to redo the burn ritual. Write down all of the reasons why you do not believe that you are extraordinary and repeat exercise six—the burning ritual.

Repeat this exercise every day until you truly believe it.

YouTube Video

"Best Motivational Video"- Speeches Compilation
Long Part 4 Posted *by*, *MotivationAndMore* **October 22, 2015.**
https://youtu.be/ZbiJ4haWoa0

Notes

Imagination

IMAGINATION IS A powerful tool that allows us to form an image of something that is not yet real. The world we live in is a world of imagination. Imagination creates reality and is a priceless gift that we all have. It is the forefront of creation. If you can imagine it, you can achieve it.

Imagining your wish fulfilled sets forth a union between your desire and the universe that helps bring it into being. Give your desire sensory vividness. Imagine what you want with as much detail as possible. Imagine you already have your desire. Daydream positively about the desire you are creating. Daydream while you are doing mundane tasks, like waiting for an appointment or standing in line, or while doing things you love, like exercising. Use every spare moment today to fantasize and dream your desires into reality.

Action

Make a wish on a star tonight. Wishing on a star is a great way to imagine your desire being put out into the universe.

There is something very sweet and powerful about gazing at a single star and making a heartfelt wish.

Use your five senses: Imagine how it feels to have your desire. What would it look like? How would it smell? How would it taste? What would you hear?

YouTube Video

"Change" Posted by "Nelson Rivera Jr", Dec. 31, 2013.
https://youtu.be/_aAA9-edO3I

Notes

LOGIC will get you from A to Z; Imagination will get you everywhere

-Albert Einstein

DAY 10

Prayer

PRAYER, SIMPLY PUT, is a conversation with God, your higher self, or whatever omnipotent power you believe in. Know that a higher power is helping you create your desires. Get into the flow. Allow what you want to flow to you. When you pray, believe that you already have what you're asking for. Send deep gratitude to your higher power for delivering your desires in the best possible way. The video listed at the end of this entry explains this action well.

Believe in a power greater than yourself. It doesn't matter what you call the greater power. Take time to connect to this power, whether it is God, your higher self, or something else.

Know in your heart that your desires are blossoming within you now. Infuse every prayer with gratitude.

Action

Pray, have an inner conversation with your higher self, God, or whatever higher powers you believe in. During this conversation, offer gratitude for all you have and for delivering your desire.

YouTube Video

"Warning: This Might Shake Up Your Belief System... Can you handle this"? Posted by "YouAreCreators." *December 9, 2013.*
https://youtu.be/UXQh05-enDs

Notes

Faith is taking the first step when you can't see the whole staircase.

-Martin Luther King

DAY 11

Creativity

EVERYONE IS BORN with creativity. Creativity is the process of bringing new ideas into being; we all have this power. Creativity allows you to transform the world. Creative people invent, imagine, and develop new things and ways of being. To unleash your creativity, you must ignite your imagination without censorship.

Doubt and fear work against creativity. Dim the part of your brain that promotes negativity and censorship. As stated above, we are all born with creativity; however, many times the regimented and formulaic education process can extinguish our natural creativity. Often times, societal pressures to conform can stifle our creativity. It takes courage to be creative.

Remember when you were a child and you played make-believe? You can give a child a cardboard box and watch them create a spaceship or a fort. That sense of wonder and creativity still lives inside of you.

Follow your heart and intuition. Allow creativity to flow through you. Be a channel for the divine and allow creative inspiration to move through you. Creativity often involves thinking outside the box.

Here are a few ideas to help you get into the creative zone.

- Watch movies or shows related to your desire that are positive and life affirming.
- Investigate positive examples of your desire on YouTube or other websites.
- Listen to music that is uplifting and elevates you toward positivity.
- Activate your heart and throat by singing out loud with feeling.
- Read positive, life-affirming books and media.
- Go outside. Nature is extremely inspirational.

- Exercise outside. Taking a walk in nature gets your blood pumping and promotes creativity.
- Let go and allow your mind to wander. Leave your phone at home in order to allow you to be in touch with your surroundings.
- Brainstorm and ignite creative thoughts. Get out a blank piece of paper and write down anything that comes to mind about your topic.

Action

Write a poem. Poetry comes from your heart.

Write your own or use the bold italicized portion of the format below:

If you look into my heart, you will see love.

I love my children, my family, my friends, and myself. I love my animals too.

If you look into my heart, you will see deep gratitude for all that has been given to me.

If you look into my heart, you will see my passion for helping others create the life of their dreams.

If you look into my heart, you will see me.

Begin your poem with the phrase "If you look into my heart, you will see…" Or create your own style of poem.

Create your poem by connecting to your heart and letting your creativity flow. Just close your eyes and feel your heart. Get into the flow and write from your heart.

YouTube Video

"The Secrets of Belief—by Ernest Holmes (Law of Attraction)." Posted by "YouAreCreators." February 8, 2013.
https://www.youtube.com/watch?v=gHRFTBRim0Q.

Notes

-unknown

DAY 12

Gratitude

GRATITUDE IS THE emotion of expressing appreciation for what you have. Practicing gratitude helps you to open your heart, feel alive, optimistic, and blissful. It also helps other people to feel seen and appreciated. Feeling grateful can boost your happiness, which can in turn change your personal vibration. You radiate and generate more positive energy when you focus on all that you have rather than on what you *think* you lack. Infuse your desire with the vibration of gratitude.

The best way to move to the next level is to have gratitude for where you are now. Gratitude is magical. It helps you see the beauty and magic that surrounds you every day.

Feel fortunate that you have the opportunity to work on what you are now creating. Thank yourself for being the powerful creator that you are. Be grateful for everything you are choosing to give yourself.

Fill every cell of your body with gratitude.

Action

Close your eyes and feel your heart. Ask yourself what you are grateful for and then write it all down. Perhaps you can start a gratitude journal. Take a moment to be deeply and truly thankful to everyone and everything that has guided you to where you are in your life.

Extra credit

Make a habit of verbally appreciating people daily.

YouTube Video

"What Gratitude Can Do for Our Lives! (Law of Attraction)." Posted by "YouAreCreators." October 27, 2014.
  https://youtu.be/CT-4Nxu2F1Y

Notes

Feeling gratitude and not expressing it is like wrapping a present and not giving it.

-William Arthur Ward

Forgiveness

FORGIVENESS IS THE conscious and deliberate decision to release feelings of resentment or vengeance towards a person who has harmed you. Forgiveness is very important because it frees you from bondage to those that you hold responsible for negative happenings in your life. It enables you to let go of anger and move on with your life.

Blaming others or yourself stops the flow of positive energy and literally holds you back from moving forward. Blame only hurts you.

Forgiveness does not mean that you need to condone the behavior of others. Forgiveness does not mean that you can't hold others responsible for their actions. To forgive means to disconnect yourself from negative emotions that you have been holding onto. Forgiveness is a gift to you. As Buddha said, "Holding on to anger is like grasping a hot coal with the intent of throwing it at someone else; you are the one who gets burned."

Take a moment and close your eyes. This time, you may activate your brain. Ask your brain who you hold resentment towards. Who in your life have you not forgiven?

Be brave and forgive. Again, forgiveness does not mean that you ever have to speak to that person again. Forgiveness means you are clearing your identity attached to the issues. Forgiveness means you are disconnecting from that person's actions completely. By deeply forgiving, you break and dissolve the cords and free yourself.

It is also very important to forgive yourself. If there is anything that you feel guilty about, figure out a way to forgive yourself. If you have wronged someone, be brave enough to admit it and ask for forgiveness.

By asking someone for forgiveness, you will free yourself as well as release them. The person may choose to forgive you and you may decide to reconnect. If the person does not forgive you, your apology will still be validating in some way to them. Either way you will be free.

Action

Write a letter to a person you are resentful towards and tell them that they are forgiven. You don't need to send the letter. If you do, wait at least forty-eight hours before sending it so that you know you're making the right decision.

If a letter does not feel right, simply visualize the person who has harmed you. With compassion, say and feel, "I forgive you. Please forgive me." Repeat this ritual until you have truly forgiven and cut the ties.

You're now free of the karma with that individual. If you still think of this individual with hatred in your heart, keep repeating the exercise until all of the resentment is cleared.

Once you have truly forgiven, you will be free to manifest what you want in your life. Remember to make peace with your past so that it won't spoil the present. "Now" is a gift!

When you get to a place where you are creating your deepest desires and living the life of your dreams, you will look back and realize that each stone on the path has lead you to where you are now.

YouTube Video

"11 Forgotten Laws—The Law of Forgiveness (Bob Proctor Law of Attraction)." Posted by "lawofattractionhelp." November 6, 2011. https://youtu.be/bExM31EBeQA

Notes

Resentment is like drinking poison and hoping your enemies get killed.

-Nelson Mandela

Activate

Now it's time for some creative fun. Activate your dreams through creative expression. The difference between a dreamer and a creator is action. Just being creative, imagining, and wanting something is not enough. You must take action towards your desire everyday.

A vision board can be created on a bulletin board or poster board. This is a place to display images that represent whatever you are creating. You can include words, phrases, affirmations, images and pictures from a magazine and other sources. Making a vision board helps you visualize your dreams.

Another creative project I like to do is during the first three days of the new Moon phase. I like to take out a blank piece of paper, light a candle, get my basket of markers, and write words and draw pictures about what I am creating. Astrologers say that the first three days of the new moon cycle is an optimum time to plant seeds for new intentions.

Stay on track with each chapter of this workbook, no matter what phase the moon is in. If you like the idea of working on an activity like this with the new moon energy, mark it in your calendar and do another creative project of your choosing during that time.

Hold excitement and gratitude in your heart as you do this next fun, creative project.

Action

Make a vision board or take out a piece of paper and a pen or markers to dream out loud on a piece of paper. Paper and pen work best as, the power of physically writing contains more energy than typing on a keyboard.

Write down what you choose to bring into your life. You can write a list, a story, a book, a poem, a song, or a mantra. You can also create a vision board. You can do all of the above activities or make up one of your own. Take the time to be quiet, listen to your heart, and let your desires flow from your hand to the paper.

YouTube Video

"Napoleon Hill Laws of Success Full Length" Love.Inspires.Faith.Empowers
   January 13, 2013.
   https://youtu.be/8EQWhQt9OQo

Notes

Dreams can come true if you have the courage to pursue them.

-Walt Disney

DAY 15

Believe

BELIEVING IS ACCEPTING something to be true. Believing in your dreams will help you shape your future. You must believe wholeheartedly that your desire is possible.

The universe has your back. The universe is a "yes machine." Send out your heart's desire, while taking action to manifest it. The universe says, "yes" to everything. If you say, "I want to meet my soul mate." The universe will say, "Yes, you want to meet your soul mate." leaving you in the same wanting space.

Instead say what you want in the progressive tense, "I am now enjoying life with my soul mate." It is a subtle but powerful difference.

You can also make space for that person or thing in your life before it appears. For example, my desire was to manifest my soul mate. I bought a home for my children and I. I placed a nightstand and reading lamp on each side of the bed. While I was remodeling my bathroom, I put in a second sink for my future husband.

Say things in the present as if they are happening now. Make space in your life for your desire. Come from a place of abundance and know that you already possess what you seek.

Action

Start a journal about your desire today. Write about it as if it is happening now. Be grateful for your desire. How will it enhance your life? How will it enhance the lives of others?

YouTube Video

"Believe in the Impossible and Make Your Dreams Come True." Posted by "Anthony Beardsell." May 28, 2015.
   https://youtu.be/Ec607-O__Iw

Notes

Rituals

A RITUAL IS an activity that is preformed for symbolic and emotional value. To make an action become a ritual, it must have symbolic meaning to you. Any action can become a personal ritual when you infuse intention. The power of ritual is in your belief. The more you believe in your ritual, the more power that ritual will have.

Do your ritual in a quiet place. You may play inspiring music if you wish. If you feel any negativity, take a moment to burn sage around your body and imagine all negative energy dissipating.

Create a sacred space to preform your ritual.

Ritual examples:

- Create an altar. An altar is a table where you can place objects or pictures that represent your desire. You can add pictures of those you love, flowers, statues, candles, smells, or images that inspire you to your altar. Look at it at least once a day for inspiration. You can also practice meditation, prayer or yoga in front of your altar.
- Meditation or prayer that is full of gratitude and intention is a super powerful ritual to do each day.
- Bath rituals are one of my favorites. Water has cleansing and clearing properties. Immerse yourself into the bath and visualize your desire. If you feel any internal or external negative energy imagine being cleared of all negativity. Relax in the bath to soothe your mind, body, and spirit. Say a prayer for the release of any energy that is not for your highest good. Ask for support to raise your personal vibration. After your bath, pull the plug and

imagine all negative energy draining down into the earth and being transformed into love.

Bliss bath:
>   One-cup baking soda
>   One-cup sea salt,
>   A few drops of organic essential oil that holds meaning or smells good to you.

Energy clearing bath:
>   One-cup apple cider vinegar
>   One-cup sea salt
>   Light a candle or create your own ritual to signify that you are going into a ritual space.

You may choose any of the rituals above or create one that is meaningful to your heart.

Action

Complete your own ritual today. You may create your own or use one of the above. A hot bath with sea salt and a candle is always a great ritual. Remember to infuse belief into your ritual to activate it.

YouTube Video

"New Moon Magic- Recharge "- Igniting The Sacred Posted by "Igniting the sacred", January 10, 2016.
>   https://youtu.be/Jx_ZS2PfzG4

Notes

Magic happens when you believe

-unknown

DAY 17

Meditation

MEDITATION HELPS YOU to access your subconscious mind. When you meditate, you quiet your conscious mind. This enables you to enter a deep place of inner peace. Meditation increases your energy and ability to create your dreams into reality. You may use any positive, life-affirming meditations that work for you. Any kind of meditation practice will get the job done.

I really like guided meditations and yoga nidra. These allow you to lie down, relax, and follow the voice of the person guiding the process. It is the easiest form of meditation for beginners.

I have created a few meditations that you can download on my website (www.dreamoutloud.vision) or listen to them YouTube. My favorite time to practice guided meditation is in the afternoon when I feel tired. After fifteen minutes of meditation, I feel energized and inspired.

Meditating helps clear your mind and relax your body. It helps you connect with your subconscious mind. Guided meditation allows you to plant seeds to help you manifest with ease. Try a few and find the meditations that resonate with you the most. You can do the same meditation every day or switch it up. If there's something you're working on, search for it on YouTube. You can search for videos such as, "guided meditation for positive energy" or "meditation for love."

Action
Meditate today.

Extra Credit

Begin a daily meditation practice, even if it's just five minutes per day.

YouTube Video

"New moon manifesting and abundance guided meditation". Posted by, "Husky Light"
    July 14, 2015.
    https://youtu.be/yeKZTaBvRfc
    Or

"Bob Proctor- Abundance Meditation"
    Posted by "Proctor TV" on March 12, 2015.
    https://youtu.be/Ee_Z4b449N4

Notes

Quiet your mind and your soul will speak.

- Ma Jaya Sati Bhagavati

Visualize

VISUALIZATION IS AN integral part of the manifestation process. Visualizing means painting a vivid picture in your mind of the reality you are creating. The easier you can visualize, the faster your desire will flow to you.

Visualize your dreams happening now! Let's say you want a new car. Visualize the car you want. Imagine yourself sitting inside of that car. What color is it? What is the interior like? Imagine you can smell the leather seats. Imagine yourself driving on your favorite road in your new car. See yourself driving home in your new car and parking in your garage or driveway. The more clearly you can see your desire, the easier you can achieve it. You must believe in your desires to activate them.

Feel in your heart that what you want is already happening. Feel yourself already having or being what you desire. This will unleash your power to make it so.

Action

Write your desire on three note cards. Place one by your bed, one in your wallet and the other somewhere that you will be inclined to see it.

Read your manifestation card each morning upon waking, during the day, and each night before you go to sleep. Feel joy in your heart as you imagine your desire happening in the present.

YouTube Video

"All Thought Is Creative, The Powers of the Mind! (Law of Attraction)." Posted by "YouAreCreators." May 28, 2015. https://youtu.be/HqD8RtyUU00.

Notes

If you can imagine it and visualize it, you can create it.

– Unknown

Faith

FAITH IS ONE of the most magical powers in the universe. Faith is defined as belief with strong conviction. It is a firm belief in something in which there may be no tangible proof. It is a deep feeling of knowing. Faith speaks the language of the heart. It is an expression that goes beyond the conscious mind. Faith is a combination of desire, belief, trust, and expectation.

Faith is the opposite of doubt. If your fear is stronger than your faith you will dramatically slow down your ability to create your desire. It's almost impossible to manifest if you don't have faith.

Connect to a higher power. No matter what religion you practice, connect to your source, whether it is God, nature, deities, or your higher self.

Faith is an active ingredient that helps you create your dreams quickly and for your highest good. Know that your source is working with you and through you to manifest your dreams. Feel and allow this higher power to support you.

Pray daily to your source with gratitude in your heart for all you have, all you have created so far, and for co-creating your heart's desire now.

Action

Write a paragraph or more about your faith in yourself. If you wish, you can also write about your faith in a higher power.

Write gratitude notes to yourself and the universe for fulfilling your desires. Mail them to yourself. You can open them immediately when they arrive, or wait to open them when you need extra encouragement.

YouTube Video

"Fear or Faith? You choose...(Law Of Attraction)" Posted by,"YouAreCreators."
May 10, 2013.
https://youtu.be/8kWQOLdZCjE

Notes

- unknown

Action

Action is the key to manifesting your dreams into reality.

Here is an example. When I started Lifestyle Fitness, I wanted more clients. I sat down to manifest. I created a flyer with my picture, phone number and services. I took copies of the flyer to health-food stores and community boards. Each time I'd hang up flyers, I'd get a new client. Interestingly, when I asked the person how he or she heard about me, it was usually from sources unrelated to the flyer.

Taking action for action's sake tells the universe that you're serious about what you want and helps your desire flow to you in the best way.

Without action, manifesting your heart's desire will only be a wish. Action brings it into reality.

This does not mean sitting back, wishing, and then wondering why you're not getting what you want.

Just reading this workbook is not enough. It is important to complete the action steps or create your own daily actions.

The magic is in your thoughts, intentions, and heart. Quiet the part of your brain that always fears change. Believe that the universe supports you, but just as importantly, you must take *action*.

Give your desires at least one hour per day of action energy, even if it is reading something on your topic or listening to YouTube videos about your desire. If you give your desire one hour per day for twenty-one continuous days, you will be amazed at how much closer you will get to your desire. It's also possible that you will have already manifested it before the end of twenty-one days.

Action

Take one hundred percent responsibility for your life. Ask the universe, "What do I need to do today to activate my desire?"

Listen to your heart.

Write down what comes to you.

You must follow this guidance with action. For at least one hour per day, follow your heart's instructions for accelerated manifestation.

As the writer Rumi said, "That which you seek is seeking you."

Feel gratitude and know that your desire is already happening.

YouTube Video

"When to take action using "The Law Of Attraction" (Use This!) Posted by, "YouAreCreators" August 3, 2015.
https://youtu.be/nAl3aSMXcVs

Notes

Desire without Action is merely a Daydream.

~ Tara Dale

Emotion

EMOTIONS, SUCH AS love, joy, anger or fear, are strong feelings. Emotions activate the nervous system. Your thoughts create emotions, emotions influence behavior, and behavior create your actions. When your thoughts are infused with positive emotions, they are more powerful.

Emotion is energy in motion. Think about emotion like e-mail, a vehicle of energy. E-mail is invisible mail delivered through digital energy. We all embody the power of emotion. You have an invisible force that is powerful enough to make you superhuman.

Emotions can create stress and disease as well as happiness and bliss, depending on whether your emotions are negative or positive. When you harness the power of control, your emotions will have the power to create your heart's desire. As humans, we are driven primarily by fear and love. You have a physical body and an energy body. Emotions are the energy bodies. When you can harness that energy and use it consciously as well as unconsciously, you will be able to do anything.

Your heart has a consciousness that is aware of your desires. Turn your magnetism into high gear by loving what you're creating. Genuinely and unconditionally love your desires.

Get excited about your desire. Celebrate what you want to create as if it's already in your life. By loving and celebrating what you are creating, you increase the speed at which that event will happen. It's also much more fun to do anything when love and celebration are present.

Emotions influence everything. Use your positive emotions to create your reality. Create your vision with the emotion of love, as well as with other positive emotions.

Positive thoughts and feelings help your desires move faster to you. You hold an invisible force that can make you a powerful creator. Your emotions are one of the powers of your magic wand.

Create your life with positive emotion, action, faith, and belief.

Infuse with your desires with emotion. Get excited about knowing that you have manifested your desire. Believe it is happening now.

Whatever you desire is created by the positive energy you send out. What you send out, you will create. If you believe in your heart that your desire is happening, it will! See your desires as if they are already happening, take action, and be grateful.

Action

Each day, write down the action steps that you have taken toward your dream, goal, or manifestation.

YouTube Video

"The Power Of The Heart And How It Affects Our Energy"! - By.Gregg Braden (Powerful!) Posted by, YouAreCreators, January 1, 2015
https://youtu.be/-k0LA5w9W_Y

Notes

Emotion is energy in motion

- unknown

Letter from Tara Dale

Today is the day to commit one hour of each day to doing something towards your desire. Commit to spending at least one hour for the next twenty-one days to doing something that supports your desire. If you need help with inspiration, search for your topic on YouTube and watch some videos. Listen for a few minutes, and if the video doesn't resonate, move on to another one.

At the beginning of your journey, write a description about what you are manifesting. Remember to write it in the positive. Number each day one through twenty-one. If you have not yet reached you goal, keep giving it at least one hour a day of love and action for at least twenty-one days. Each day, write about what actions you have taken towards your desire.

Write down any inspiration that you receive. If doubt creeps in, you can always repeat the burn ceremony from chapter six. Do something towards your desire daily. If you have to skip a day, continue the next day.

I would love to hear any feedback on this workbook during your process. I would also love to hear what you are creating and what you have accomplished so far. My e-mail is, *Dreamoutloudwithtara@gmail.com.*

Take out your magic wand and enjoy creating your Heart's desires!

I wish you many blessings on your path. May this workbook inspire you to create the life you truly desire. May you have the courage to listen to your heart and create the life of your dreams!

Love,

Tara

Author Biography

Tara Dale is the cofounder of *Yoga Tree*, a chain of yoga studios in the San Francisco area, that provide workshops and a teacher training center with offerings from top instructors from around the world.

Tara is now writing books about manifesting your heart's desires. She is also creating an app for guided meditation. You can listen to many of her guided meditations her YouTube channel, *Dream out loud with Tara*.

Tara grew up competing in various riding competitions in St. Louis, Missouri. She attended the University of Arizona, graduating with a degree in media arts and communication. After brief stints in advertising and event planning, she decided to follow her passion for fitness and yoga and launched her own studio the *Inner Garden*. A few years later, she opened her first of nine yoga studios called *Yoga Tree*.

Dale ultimately wrote, "Dream Out Loud" to help others break free of the small, boxed-up reality they may have settled for and realize their heart's desires.

Thank you to all of the incredible speakers and leaders for allowing me to post your inspiring YouTube videos to this workbook.
Thank you to all of the speakers, past and present, for your inspiration!

Anthony Beardsell
Bob Proctor
Donald Walsh
Florence Scovel Shinn
Husky Light
Igniting the sacred
John Assaraf
John Kehoe
Motivation and more
Nelson Rivera Jr
Napoleon Hill
Sonia Chochette
U.S. Anderson
You Are Creators

Thank you Harriet for all of your inspiring illustrations inside each chapter!

CPSIA information can be obtained at www.ICGtesting.com
Printed in the USA
LVOW09s1030240816

501651LV00006B/166/P